HANDS-ON ECOLOGY

By Ovid K. Wong, Ph.D.

GRADY MIDDLE SCHOOL LIBRARY

CHILDRENS PRESS®
CHICAGO

This book is dedicated to MR. AND MRS. CECIL HU, my
father-in-law and mother-in-law.

Library of Congress Cataloging-in-Publication Data

Hands-on ecology / by Ovid Wong
  p.   cm.
Includes index.
Summary: Presents activities to explore and emphasize ecology and to demonstrate practical ways of conserving the environment.
ISBN 0-516-00539-1
1. Ecology—Experiments—Juvenile literature. 2. Environmental education—Activity programs—Juvenile literature. 3. Environmental protection—Experiments—Juvenile literature. [1. Ecology—Experiments. 2. Environmental protection—Experiments. 3. Experiments.] I. Title.
QH541.24.W66   1991   91-12751
574.5'078—dc20   CIP
                                 AC

PHOTO CREDITS

AP/Wide World Photos—8 (bottom), 59, 75, 79
© Cameramann International Ltd.—Cover, 7, 10, 16, 19, 21, 23, 27, 31, 37, 38, 40, 43, 45, 46, 47 (2 photos), 48, 50, 51, 52, 53, 54, 56, 60, 61, 62, 64, 70, 72, 74, 77, 83, 84, 86, 87, 93, 95, 97, 99, 100, 103, 105, 107, 109, 111, 114, 115, 119, 120
© Norma Morrison—94 (center right)
NASA—3, 13, 116
Tony Stone Worldwide/Chicago—© Steve Elmore, 90; © Chuck Keeler, 94 (center left); © Gerald Herbeck, 94 (bottom)
Valan—© R. Moller, 8 (top); © Francis Lépine, 28; © John Cancalosi, 33; © Aubrey Lang, 34; © J.A. Wilkinson, 89, 94 (top)
All illustrations by Charles Hills

Copyright © 1991 by Childrens Press®, Inc.
All rights reserved. Published simultaneously in Canada.
Printed in the United States of America.
1 2 3 4 5 6 7 8 9 10 R 00 99 98 97 96 95 94 93 92 91

TABLE OF CONTENTS

Introduction 9

Chapter 1	**Principles of Ecology** 11	

       How Do We Make Decisions About the Basic Needs of Life? 12
       How Does the Availability of Needs Affect
           Populations? 15
       What Is the Evidence of Wildlife Interacting
           With the Environment? 18
       What Is the Carrying Capacity of the Environment? 22
       What Do Owls Need From the Environment to Survive? 26
       How Do Plants Contribute to Human Needs? 30
       What Animals Are Extinct or Endangered? 32
       How Do Animals and Plants Live Interdependently
           in the Environment? 36

Chapter 2   **Operation Clean Air** 44
       How Clean Is the Air? 47
       What Are the Effects of Polluted Air? 50
       How Do Filters Help to Clean Air? 54
       How Does Cigarette Smoke Pollute Your Internal
           Environment? 56
       What Is the Greenhouse Effect? 60
       How Can We Reduce the Risk of Radon Poisoning? 62

Chapter 3	**Operation Clean Water** 65	
	Is Your Drinking Water Free From Pollutants? 66	
	How Do You Clean Water? 72	
	How Does an Ocean Oil Spill Affect Wildlife? 76	
Chapter 4	**Operation Clean Land** 80	
	What Is a Landfill and Why Are Landfills Becoming a Problem? 82	
	How Can Some Substances Be Toxic to Living Things? 85	
	What Are a Farmer's Alternatives to Using Toxic Chemicals? 88	
Chapter 5	**Save the Earth: Recycle** 91	
	How Can Paper Be Recycled? 92	
	What Can Be Recycled and What Cannot? 96	
Chapter 6	**Save the Earth: Conserve and Use Clean Energy** 98	
	What Kind of Energy User Are You? 100	
	How Can You Conserve Energy in Your Home? 104	
	What Is Solar Energy? 106	
	What Is Solar Distillation? 108	
	How Can You Heat Water With Solar Energy? 112	
Chapter 7	**Action: Putting It All Together** 117	
	Have You Hugged Your Planet Today? 118	

Words You Should Know 122
Index 123
About the Author 126

SOURCES OF MATERIALS

Most of the materials listed in this book may be purchased from your local hardware store or supermarket. Live materials may be purchased from pet stores and bait shops. However, some special materials may also be ordered from the following sources:

Carolina Biological Supply Company
Burlington, North Carolina 27215
(800) 632-1231

Fisher Scientific Company
4901 W. LeMoyne Street
Chicago, IL 60651
(800) 621-4769

NASCO West Inc.
P.O. Box 3837
Modesto, CA 95352
(209) 529-6957

DELTA Education
P.O. Box 915
Hudson, NH 03061
(800) 258-1302

Introduction

David and Lori love the great outdoors. They have spent many happy hours fishing in clean, sparkling water teeming with wildlife, and boating under the clear blue skies. But David and Lori can no longer enjoy the outdoors. Sooty smoke from a huge oil refinery in town produced acid rain — the chemicals from the smoke combined with the moisture in the air. Worst of all, an accident has turned the area into a nightmare. A giant oil tanker ran aground and leaked thick, tarry oil, polluting many miles of water. In just a short time, the livelihood of the community was threatened because of the damage to fisheries, agriculture, and tourism. And the true extent of the damage may not be known for years!

What you have read is not make-believe. Environmental disasters destroy natural resources and threaten human survival. Many people are beginning to understand that we cannot live apart from our environment. We depend on it for our livelihood and well-being.

The information in this book is reinforced by hands-on activities. Together, they will help you make wise decisions and take action to protect our precious and fragile environment. Remember that humans are responsible for many environmental problems, and we can all work to solve them. You can help. Welcome to Hands-On Ecology!

Chapter 1

Principles of Ecology

*No living thing is an island, entire of itself.
Everything is a piece of the environment, a
part of the planet Earth.*
—An ecologist

This statement strongly affirms the interdependence of all living things, including humans, with the environment. Ecologists are scientists who study the relationships between living things and the environment. They stress repeatedly that we cannot afford to abuse the environment that provides us with air, water, food, and space—the basic needs of life.

How Do We Make Decisions About the Basic Needs of Life?

Materials
none needed

Procedure
1. Read the following story carefully. You will need the information to make some important decisions.

   A spaceship is marooned far out in space as a result of engine failure. The astronauts radio Earth asking for help, but they learn that it will take fourteen days for another spaceship to reach them with assistance. They check their supplies. Their supply of air seems to be sufficient for fourteen days. But they have enough food to support normal activity for only ten days, and enough water for only seven days of normal living. The more energetic their activities are, the faster their life-support elements will run out. The stranded astronauts must make important decisions about their survival.

2. Play the role of the stranded astronauts. You and your team must decide how the astronauts will share their limited supply of air, food, and water. You can establish rules and priorities for conserving the resources in such a way that everybody will survive until help arrives. Remember, you are making group decisions instead of individual decisions.

3. Use the following guidelines.

Ideas to conserve air	Priority
Ideas to conserve food	Priority
Ideas to conserve water	Priority

Conclusion
The decisions about what to do on a marooned spaceship will vary according to various priorities and differing values. You may pick up good ideas—and thus make good decisions—by sharing your ideas with others.

Think and Explore
1. On the basis of what you learned in the activity, which requirement for living is most important—air, food, or water?
2. How do you compare the limited resources on the marooned spaceship to the limited resources on planet Earth?
3. How do you contrast the importance of conserving resources on the marooned spaceship to conserving resources on planet Earth?
4. What are the important factors in making good decisions?

How Does the Availability of Needs Affect Populations?

(You will need 11 people)

Materials
none needed

Procedure
1. Mark two parallel lines on the ground with at least 33 feet (10 meters) between them. Have five players stand on each line. An additional person is needed as a referee.
2. The ten players will use four hand signs to represent the basic needs of life. Two fingers pinching the nose means air. Two fingers over the lips means water. Two hands over the stomach means food. Two arms stretched straight above the head means space. Practice these hand signs until everyone knows them well.
3. Assign the five people on one line to be "hares." Assign the five people on the other line to be "basic needs of life." At the start of the activity the players on each line should stand with their backs to each other.
4. Before starting each round, each of the ten players in the game should privately decide which hand sign—over the nose, the lips, the stomach, or the head—he or she will use.

> DO THIS ACTIVITY UNDER AN ADULT'S SUPERVISION

5. On the count of three by the referee, everybody turns around with their hand signs in place. (Players may not change hand signals after the count.) Each "hare" looks for a "basic needs" person with the same hand sign and brings that person back to the "hare" line. In other words, "hares" with a water sign run to a "basic needs" with a water sign, air to air, space to space, and food to food. The "basic needs" people do not move unless they are taken by the "hares."
6. "Hares" that find a "basic needs" person survive the round. Two "hares" might go for the same "basic need," but only the "hare" who gets the "basic need" survives. Those who do not survive, die and leave the game.
7. Repeat the activity for ten rounds. Let the referee keep track of the number of "hares" that survive each round on a chart like the one shown. A bar or line graph may be constructed.

Conclusions

1. The number of "hares" that survive over the ten rounds represents the change in a natural animal population over a period of ten years. The number of animals that survive each year depends on what basic needs of life are available in the environment.
2. The availability of the basic needs of life limits the size of the animal population. If the basic needs of life are not met, more animals will die, and the population will decrease.

Think and Explore

A scientist found that a great number of hares died of a strange disease during one year. The following year, the number of mountain lions decreased. Can you explain why? Which animal is the hunter? Which is the hunted?

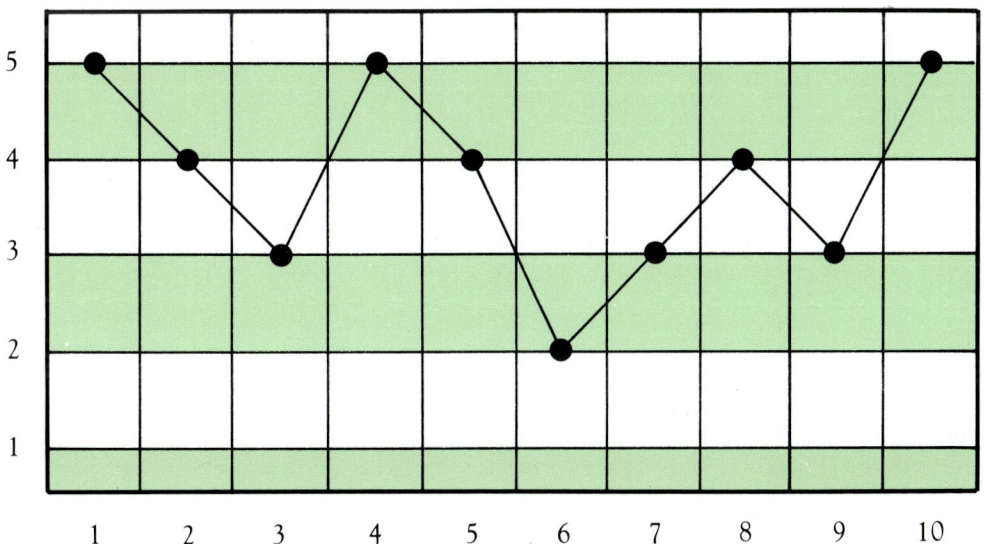

17

What Is the Evidence of Wildlife Interacting With the Environment?

Materials
plaster of paris
tin can or plastic bowl
spray can of clear plastic or shellac
stapler
thin cardboard

Procedure
1. Take a field trip to a nearby stream, lake, or forest preserve where you can find animal tracks. (You will probably find tracks where there is soft mud or sand.)
2. Locate a track and do the following steps to make a plaster cast.
3. Carefully clean the track of loose particles of soil, leaves, twigs, or other debris.
4. Spray the track with shellac or plastic from a spray can. (The thin layer of spray will help to form the bottom of the cast.)
5. Cut a strip of cardboard 2 inches (5 centimeters) wide and staple the ends together to form a ring that will fit around the track. (If necessary, use two strips stapled together.) Put the ring around the track.

> DO THIS ACTIVITY UNDER AN ADULT'S SUPERVISION

6. Mix two cups of plaster of paris in a tin can or plastic bowl by adding water slowly until the mixture has the consistency of thick cream.
7. Pour the plaster carefully into the ring, covering the track. Fill the ring all the way to the rim. Allow the plaster about 20 minutes to harden.
8. Lift the cast and remove the cardboard ring.
9. Clean the cast by scraping and washing it. Now you have lifted the track and can bring it home or to school!

Conclusion

An animal track is evidence that animals interact with the environment. For example, tracks found near a stream could mean that animals were seeking water or food from the stream.

Think and Explore

Jonathan found some animal tracks near a riverbank. The tracks consisted of big and small footprints mixed together in the same area. A little farther down the riverbank, only the big footprints could be found. Can you explain what might have happened, based on the evidence of the animal tracks?

What Is the Carrying Capacity of the Environment?

Materials
fruit-fly culture
  (available in vials from a biological supply house)
paper
pencil
small paint brush

Procedure
1. Carefully examine a fruit-fly culture to identify the four basic needs of life: air, water, food, and space.
2. Count the number of fruit flies every two days and keep a record of the number. You might find it easier to count the fruit flies when they are inactive. To make the flies inactive, you can lower the temperature of the culture by placing it in a freezer for one to two minutes. The cold temperature will slow down the fruit flies. You can even remove the plug of the culture vial and shake the immobilized insects onto a piece of paper and count them! As soon as the flies start to get active again, they should be brushed back into the vial for more refrigeration, if needed.
3. Look at your population record of fruit flies over two weeks. What changes do you see in the population? Record your findings on a chart like the one shown on page 23.

Number of Fruit Flies
60
55
50
45
40
35
30
25
20
15
10
5
0
Days
0
2
4
6
8
10
12
14

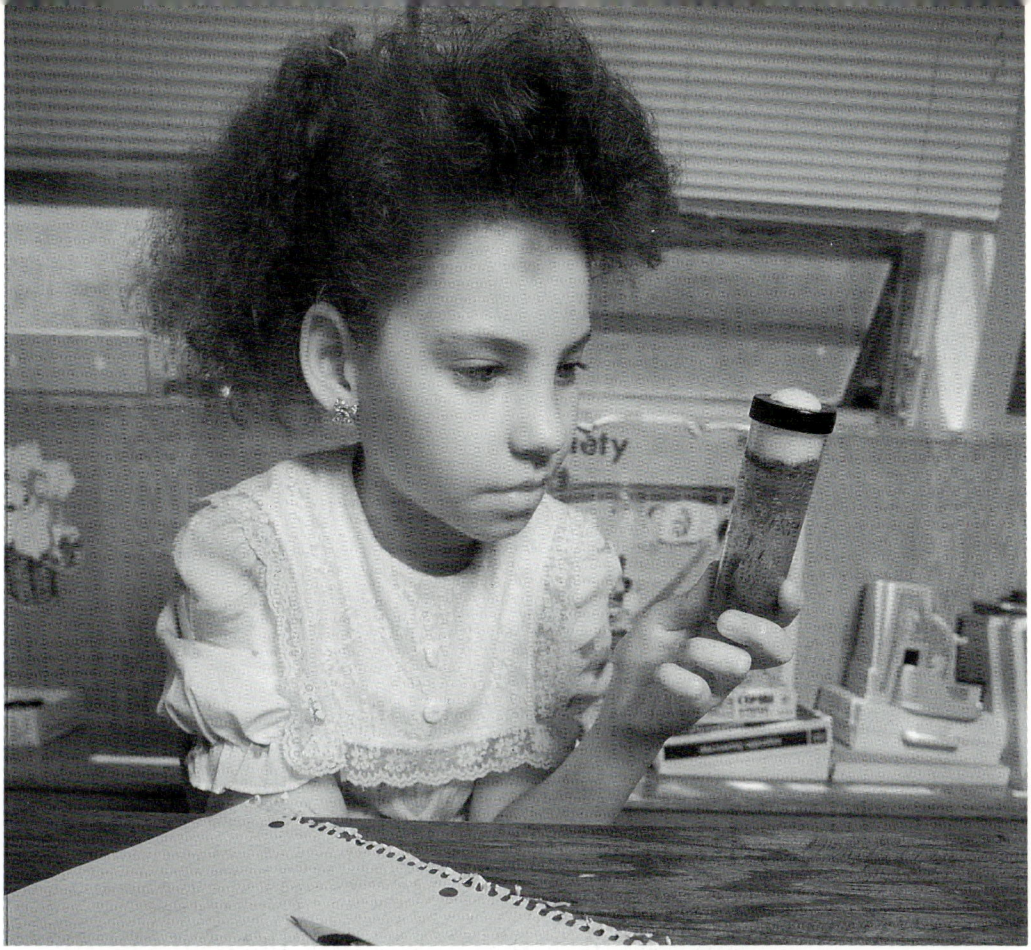

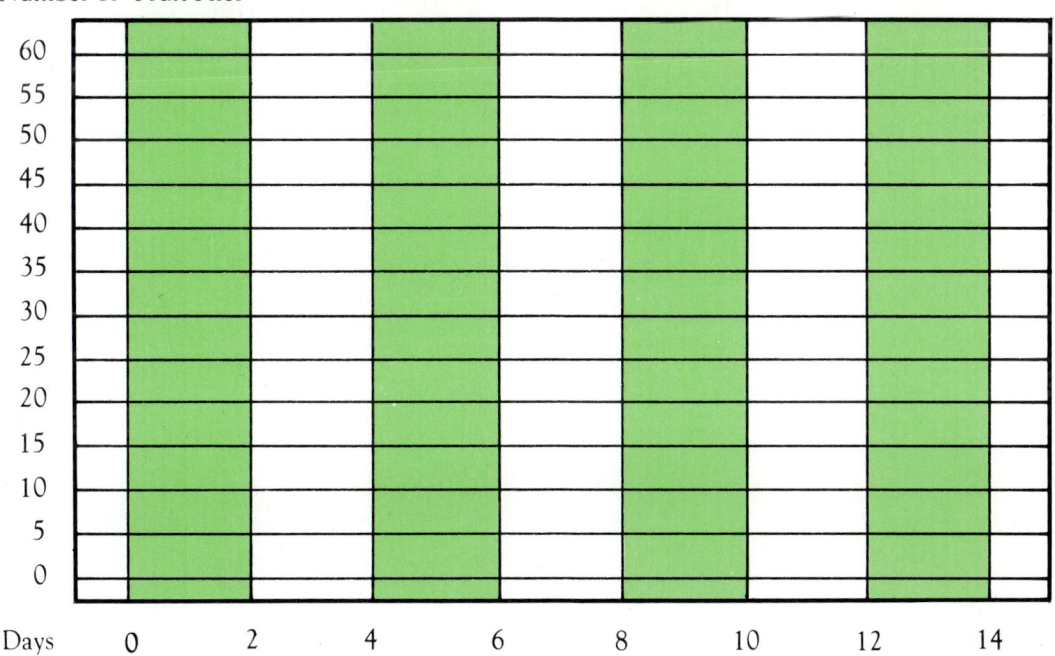

Conclusions

1. Air, food, water, and space — the basic needs of life — affect the carrying capacity of the environment. The carrying capacity is the number of organisms (plants or animals) that an environment can support at any one time.
2. In the fruit fly experiment, the supply of air is unlimited, because the culture vial is connected to the outside world by a porous plug. A porous plug allows air to get in and out. However, the food, the space, and the water (from the food medium) are very limited. As the fruit flies increase by natural reproduction, the demand on the basic needs of the environment increases. Consequently, the population increases beyond the carrying capacity of the fruit-fly environment. Also, as the food and water are consumed, the carrying capacity of the environment decreases.
3. The changes in the fruit-fly population are quite dramatic if the fruit-fly numbers are plotted on a graph.

Think and Explore
1. Do you think the data from the fruit-fly experiment reflects changes in the human population of the world? What are the similarities? What are the differences?
2. Suggest one thing people can do to increase the carrying capacity of their environment? Can you explain?
3. Extend the experiment beyond the 2-week limit to six weeks. What happens to the fruit-fly population?

What Do Owls Need From the Environment to Survive?

Materials
owl pellets
   (may be obtained from a biological supply house)
toothpicks
tweezers
poster board
glue

Procedure
1. Owls usually swallow their prey whole. The fur and bones of the prey are not digested and are regurgitated about 12 hours after the meal in the form of a pellet. You can obtain owl pellets from a biological supply house. Each pellet will be about 2 inches (5 centimeters) long, with a diameter of about 1 inch (2.5 centimeters). The pellet, which usually comes wrapped in foil is clean and odorless.
2. Remove the foil. Use the toothpicks to carefully separate the fur and other debris from the small animal bones.
3. Sort the bones into groups and lay them on a piece of paper. The diagram can help you identify the bones. The skulls will be the most obvious pieces in the pellet.
4. Put the bones together with the help of the diagram, and if you have all the bones, you can reconstruct a complete skeleton. Glue the skeleton on a piece of poster board for display.

Conclusions
1. The remains of small animals found in owl pellets indicate that the owl is a bird of prey. Owls interact with the environment to obtain food to live.
2. The contents of the pellets show that the hunter preys on the hunted to live, simple evidence of the food chain.

Think and Explore

1. How can a scientist use the owl-pellet data to identify the different small animal species living in a specific area?
2. Can you suggest natural places in your area where owl pellets might be located? What do you need to know about a place before you go on an owl-pellet hunt?

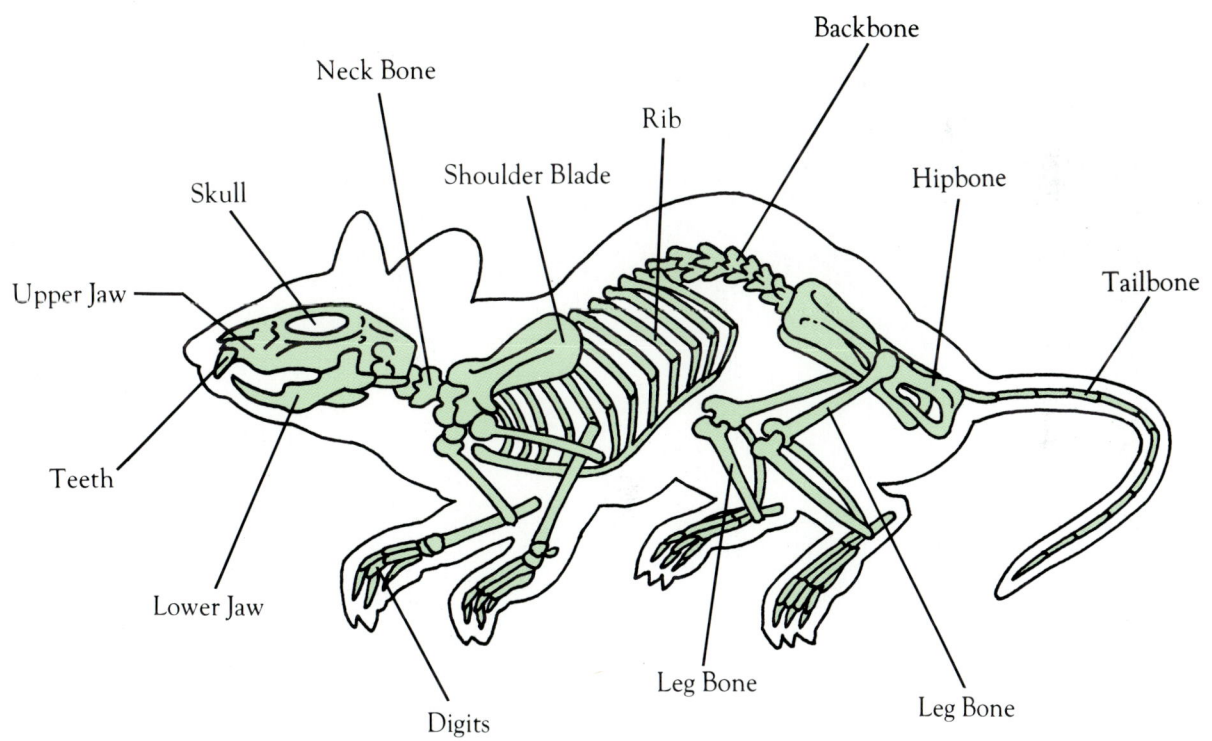

How Do Plants Contribute to Human Needs?

Materials
paper
pencil

Procedure
1. Collect a number of common items that people use or eat every day. These items can be a shoe, an apple, a cotton towel, a wooden spoon, and so on.
2. Trace the history of each item in your collection all the way back to its origin. Construct a flow chart like the following to record your data:
   (a) shoe←store←factory←tannery←stockyard←farm←cow←feed←plants
   (b) chair←store←factory←lumber←trees←plants

   You may ask a friend to share this activity and see who can be first to trace the origin of an item.

Conclusion
How many of your items have their origin in plants? Plants are one of our most important natural resources. People get food, clothes, and building materials—directly and indirectly—from plants.

Think and Explore
1. People cut down trees (plants) to get materials that improve the quality of their lives. What would be one major impact on the environment if the trees of the world were overly exploited?
2. Many items found in the home, such as nylon stockings, food packaging, and other plastics do not originate with plants. Find out the origin of these items.

What Animals Are Extinct or Endangered?

Materials
none needed

Procedure

1. Write a letter to ask for a list of extinct and endangered species of animals. You can also ask why some animals are extinct or endangered. Lists of endangered species can be obtained from:

   Director, Office of Endangered Species
   U.S. Fish and Wildlife Service
   U.S. Department of the Interior
   Washington, DC 20240

   World Wildlife Fund
   1250 24th Street N.W.
   Washington, D.C. 20037

2. Enter the animals' names in a chart like the following and make a check in the appropriate column.

	Animal	Extinct	Endangered	Reasons
(a)				
(b)				
(c)				
(d)				
(e)				

3. You may further classify the animals into smaller groups, such as mammals, birds, reptiles, and insects.

Conclusions
1. Extinct animals are species that have died out completely, like dinosaurs. Endangered species, on the other hand, are animals at risk of becoming extinct. The giant panda, the wood bison, and the blue whale are all endangered animals.

2. Many organisms are threatened with becoming endangered—and finally extinct—because of major impacts on the environment caused by such factors as overcrowding (space), polluted air and water, and overhunting by humans.

Think and Explore
The bald eagle—the national symbol of the United States—is an endangered bird. Read about the bald eagle in encyclopedias or reference books, and then propose a plan to save the bird from total extinction.

The giant panda is the symbol for the World Wildlife Fund. Read about the panda, and propose a plan to save this animal from total extinction.

How Do Animals and Plants Live Interdependently in the Environment?

> NOTE: THIS ACTIVITY IS DIVIDED INTO PARTS A, B, C, AND D.

Part A

How Can Carbon Dioxide Gas Be Detected by a Chemical Indicator?

Materials
bromothymol blue (BTB) solution
drinking straw
clear medicine vial
distilled water
medicine dropper

Procedure
1. Half-fill a clear vial with distilled water.
2. Add 12 drops of BTB solution to the water. The water will turn blue. (Add more BTB if needed to make the blue more apparent.)
3. Put the straw into the water in the vial and blow slowly into the water. Do you see a color change?

Conclusions
1. BTB is an acid indicator. In the presence of an acid, the BTB solution changes from blue (not acidic) to green (slightly acidic) to yellow (more acidic). Distilled water is neutral—it is neither acidic nor alkaline. Distilled water is used in the experiment because of its neutrality.
2. Human breath contains traces of carbon dioxide gas. When carbon dioxide is put into the distilled water, a weak carbonic acid is formed.

Think and Explore
If the vial of yellow solution is left overnight, the solution will turn blue again by the next morning. Do you know what happens? (Hint: If the yellow solution is sealed tightly with a plastic wrap, the color will remain yellow!)

Part B

Do Animals Give Off Or Take Up Carbon Dioxide Gas?

Materials
2 clear medicine vials
distilled water
water snail
bromothymol blue (BTB) solution
medicine dropper

Procedure
1. Prepare two identical vials and label one A and the other B.
2. Fill both vials with distilled water. Make sure that the same amount is poured into both vials.
3. Add drops of the BTB solution to vial A to make the water blue. Do the same to vial B.
4. Put a water snail in vial A but not in vial B. Cover both vials with caps or plastic wrap.
5. The next day, observe any color change in the water. Compare the color of the water in vial A with vial B.

Conclusion
The water in vial B remains the same color. The color change in vial A indicates the presence of an acid, namely carbonic acid, which is formed by the carbon dioxide gas exhaled, or respired, by the snail. Snails and other animals, including humans, exhale carbon dioxide gas as a by-product of breathing.

Think and Explore
1. What is the purpose of setting up vial B in the experiment? (Hint: Vial B is the control of the experiment. What is the purpose of a control?)
2. Is excessive carbon dioxide in the environment (the vial) harmful to the snail? How can you find out?

Part C

Do Plants Give Off or Take Up Carbon Dioxide Gas?

Materials
2 clear medicine vials
distilled water
a water plant such as a sprig of hornwort
bromothymol blue (BTB) solution
medicine dropper

Procedure
1. Fill two identical vials with distilled water. Label one vial A and the other B. Make sure that the same amount is poured into both vials.
2. Add drops of the BTB solution to both vials to make the water blue.
3. Put a sprig of hornwort in vial A and nothing in vial B. Cover both vials with caps or plastic wrap and place the vials in a well-lighted area.
4. The next day, observe any color change in the water. Compare the color of the water in vial A with vial B.

Conclusion
The color of the water in vial A indicates the absence of any acid. What is the color change? The hornwort in vial A does not give off or produce carbon dioxide gas. For that reason, carbonic acid will not be formed. Is there a color change in B? (Vial B is the control of the experiment.)

Think and Explore
If vial A (with the hornwort) is capped and left overnight, the color of the water will change from blue to green or yellow. Can you explain why? (Hint: Plants function a little differently during the night than they do in the daylight.)

Part D

How Do Animals and Plants Balance the Production of Carbon Dioxide in the Environment?

Materials
water snails
hornwort
clear medicine vial
bromothymol blue (BTB) solution
medicine dropper

Procedure
1. Prepare a clean vial and fill it with distilled water.
2. Put enough drops of the BTB solution in the vial to make the water blue.
3. Put a water snail in the vial. (Remember, in Part A of this experiment, the blue water turned yellow because the snail was producing carbon dioxide.)
4. Put a sprig of hornwort in the vial with the snail. Then cap the vial or cover it with plastic wrap and put the vial in a well-lighted area such as a windowsill. What is your prediction? Will there be a color change?

Conclusion
The snail and the hornwort together should not produce any color change in the water. (You might

need to adjust the number of snails and the amount of hornwort in this experiment to produce this result.) What happens to the carbon dioxide gas that is produced by the snail? The gas is absorbed, or taken in, by the hornwort. This is a delicate balance of gaseous exchange between the animal and the plant in a confined environment. The gaseous exchange can be represented by the following sequence:

Animals→Carbon dioxide→Plants

Think and Explore
Many trees in the Amazon rain forest are being destroyed to clear land for ranching and farming. From what you learned in this experiment, can you explain how the disappearance of the rain forest would affect the gases in the atmosphere?

Chapter 2

Operation Clean Air

The atmosphere is a blanket of air that completely surrounds the Earth. The atmosphere is what makes life on Earth possible. Air is vital to life and to the environment because, without air, almost every animal on Earth would suffocate and die in a matter of minutes. Green plants could not live without the carbon dioxide from the air that they use to make their food. The atmosphere protects people and animals from the harmful rays of the sun. It protects us from burning up in the full heat of the sun during the day. At night, it holds in heat to help keep us from freezing. All the weather, including the rain and snow that provide the Earth with water, occurs in the lower levels of the atmosphere.

The air that we breathe today is not as clean as the air breathed by our grandparents and great grandparents. Undesirable gases and tiny bits of matter called pollutants are being released into the atmosphere, where they create air pollution. Scientists estimate that over 300 million tons (270 million metric tons) of pollutants are added to the air by North Americans every year. Many of these pollutants come from automobile exhausts. Other sources of air pollution are fossil fuels burned in factories, the burning of garbage, forest fires, and the propellants used in some spray cans. Since life depends so much on clean air, any threat to the balance of the elements in the atmosphere is a threat to the existence of all living things on this planet. We need clean air!

How Clean Is the Air?

Materials
waxed paper
scissors
petroleum jelly
adhesive tape
magnifier

Procedure
1. Cut several strips of waxed paper measuring 1 x 2½ inches (2.5 x 6.5 centimeters).
2. Smear a thin layer of petroleum jelly on each waxed-paper strip.
3. Place the strips in different locations and secure them with adhesive tape. (Strips can be placed in the kitchen, the classroom, or a bedroom. Outdoors, put them under a tree, near a park, or close to a road with heavy traffic.) Label each strip with the name of its location. Leave the

strips at the locations for one week.
4. Collect all the waxed-paper strips. Place the strips over a piece of white paper for close examination with a magnifier. What do you see? Are all the strips the same? How are they different?

Conclusion

Air pollutants adhere to the sticky surface of petroleum jelly, making the waxed-paper strip dirty. The amount of pollutants on each strip, as shown by the relative shades of gray to dark gray, indicates the condition of the air at that location.

Think and Explore

1. Can air pollution be affected by weather conditions? Prepare two waxed-paper strips coated with petroleum jelly. Place one strip in an outdoor location on a cool, dry day. Label it "Cool and Dry." Place the other strip at the same location on a hot, humid day. Label it "Hot and Humid." Then compare the pollutants on the two strips.
2. Based on the air-pollution data, where are the locations with the worst air pollution in your community?

What Are the Effects of Polluted Air?

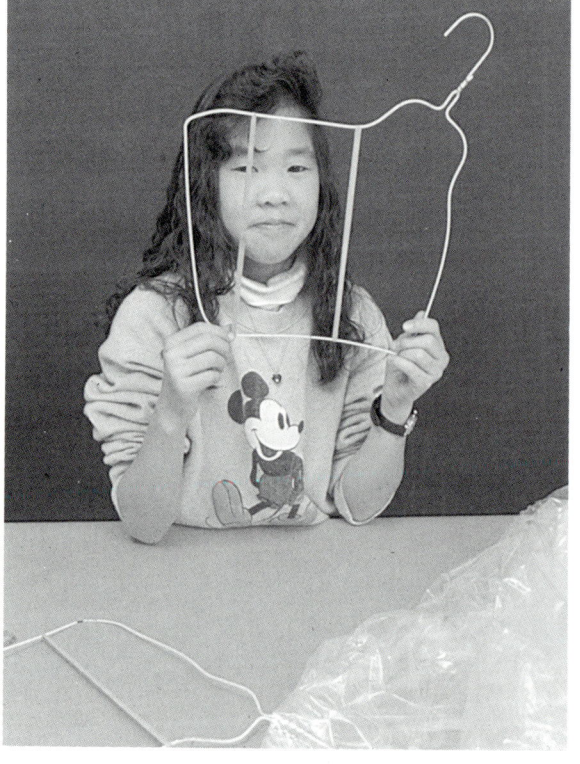

Materials
rubber bands
   (natural rubber)
2 wire coat hangers
plastic bag
magnifier

Procedure
1. Bend two wire coat hangers into the shape of a rectangle.
2. Slide two rubber bands onto each coat hanger. Make sure that the rubber bands are stretched tightly on the coat hangers. (If you are using smaller rubber bands, connect them together to fit the hanger.)

NOTE: THIS ACTIVITY WILL GIVE YOU DRAMATIC RESULTS IF YOU LIVE IN A PLACE WITH SEVERE AIR-POLLUTION PROBLEMS.

3. Put one coat hanger outdoors away from direct sunlight.
4. Put the second hanger inside a tightly sealed plastic bag in a closet.
5. Leave both hangers in place for two weeks.
6. Examine the rubber bands with a magnifier. Compare the rubber bands from the two coat hangers. Do you notice a difference? (If there is no noticeable difference, repeat the experiment for two more weeks.)
7. Remove the rubber bands from the coat hanger and stretch them out. What happens?

Conclusion
If you live in a place where air pollution is a severe problem, the outdoor rubber band will break easily. Chemicals in smog, a form of air pollution, break down the material in the rubber band and make it brittle.

Think and Explore
If smog can break down materials like rubber bands, what will it probably do to animals, trees, and humans in the environment?

How Do Filters Help to Clean Air?

Materials
different air filters
   (from a car, a furnace, or a kitchen exhaust fan)
magnifier

Procedure
1. Examine new and used air filters. Air filters are used in cars, furnaces, kitchen exhaust systems, and various appliances that require air. Ask an adult to assist you in locating these filters.
2. Examine the filter with a magnifier. What is trapped in the porous filtering materials? Compare a new and used filter. What are the differences?

Conclusion
An air filter is made of porous materials used to screen or trap airborne pollutants. A used filter is dirty. When you shake an air filter that was used in a car, you can actually see the dust and other particles coming off.

Think and Explore
1. Car maintenance technicians recommend that the air filter in the carburetor be changed frequently. Can you explain why?
2. A catalytic converter is a car exhaust attachment. What is the function of the converter? What does the converter filter?
3. To help fight air pollution, the U.S. Environmental Protection Agency (EPA) was created in 1970. Find out about the Clean Air Act at your library.

How Does Cigarette Smoke Pollute Your Internal Environment?

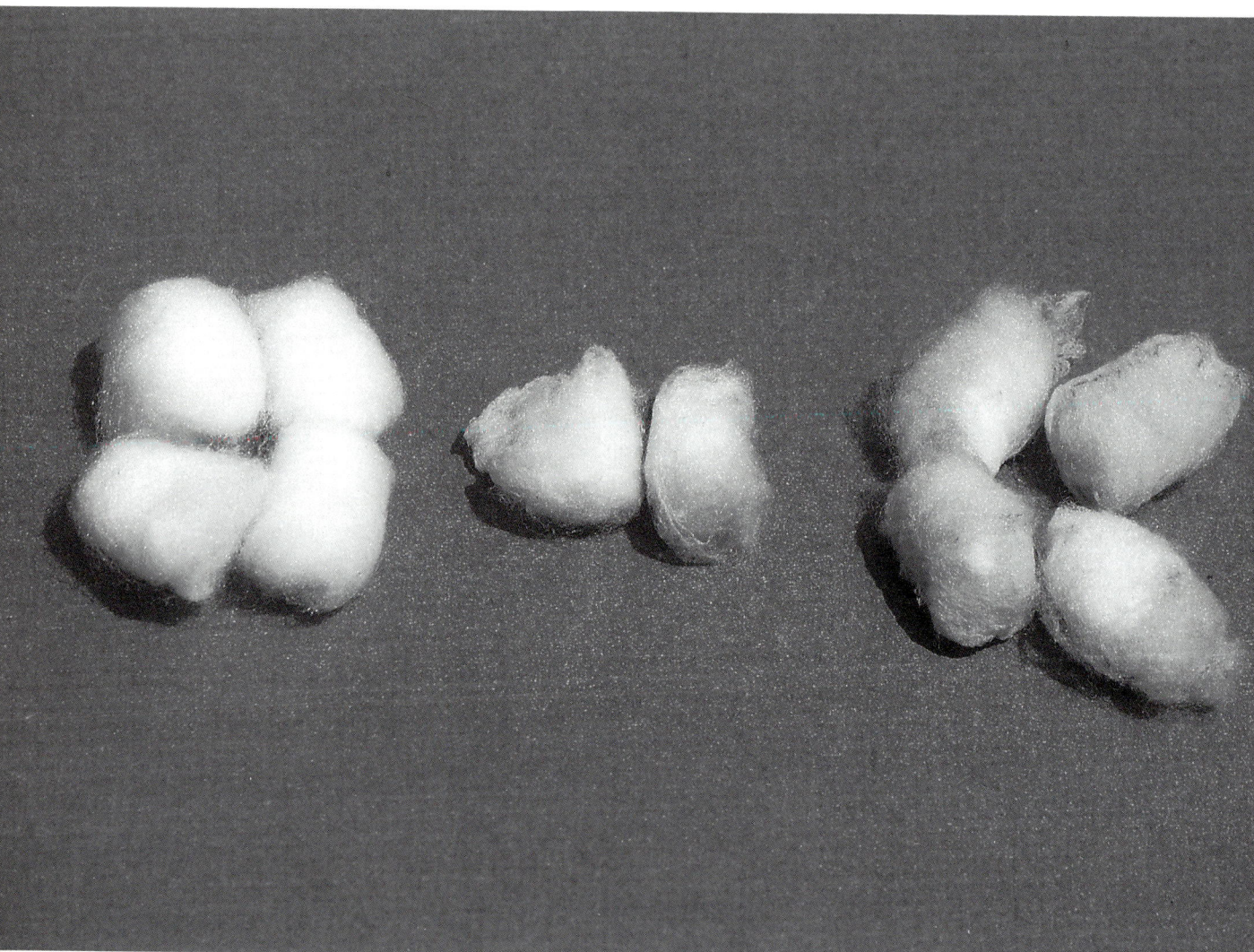

DO THIS ACTIVITY UNDER AN ADULT'S SUPERVISION

Materials
2 cigarettes (one with a filter, one without)
matches
adhesive tape
rubber tubing
glass bottle (or clear plastic bottle)
bicycle pump
2-hole rubber stopper
cotton balls

Procedure
1. Set up the equipment as shown in the diagram. Ask an adult to light the unfiltered cigarette and place it in the tube.
2. Pull the handle of the bicycle pump to draw air through the lighted unfiltered cigarette. Record your observations.
3. Clean the equipment and set up the experiment again, using a lighted *filtered* cigarette.
4. Pull the handle of the bicycle pump to draw air through the lighted filtered cigarette. Record your observations.
5. Examine and compare the cotton balls from the unfiltered cigarette experiment and the filtered cigarette experiment. Record your observations. What are the differences?

Conclusions
1. Tars from the smoked cigarettes cause the cotton balls to become discolored.
2. The discolored cotton balls used in the experiment with the filtered cigarette look a little cleaner, since some of the pollutants were trapped by the filter.

Think and Explore
1. How would you explain to a friend that cigarette smoking is dangerous to one's health?
2. Do you know what passive smoking is? Why is a passive smoker also risking the chance of getting such diseases as heart trouble or lung cancer and respiratory problems?

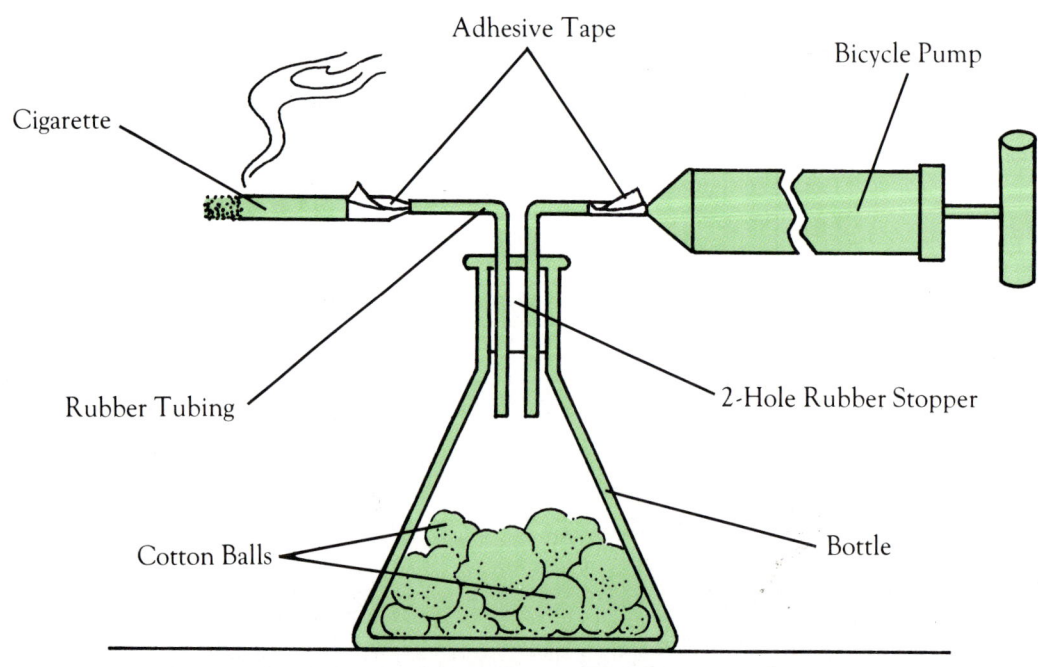

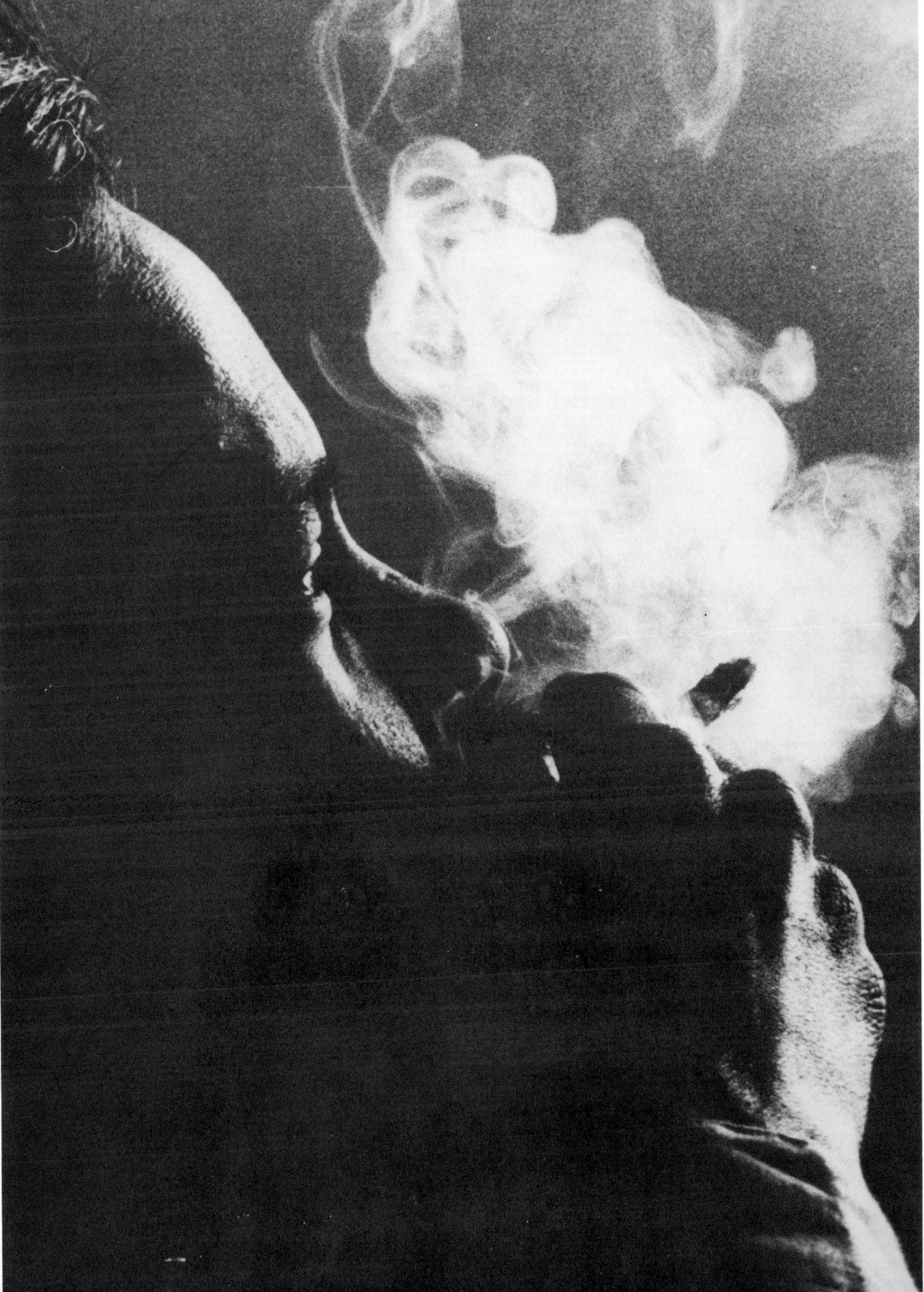

What Is the Greenhouse Effect?

Materials
2 thermometers
2 glass jars
paper
pencil

Procedure
1. Do this activity on a sunny day. Place a thermometer inside a sealed glass jar. Put another thermometer outside the jar and right next to it.
2. Put the equipment outdoors in direct sunlight.
3. Record the temperature on each thermometer once each minute until the temperature reaches its maximum.
4. Compare the data to find out:
   (a) the time it took for each thermometer to reach the maximum temperature.
   (b) the rate of temperature increase (which thermometer showed a greater rise per minute).

Conclusions
1. The air temperature inside the glass jar will be higher than the air temperature outside, due to the heat trapped inside the sealed container. In a similar way, the increased amount of carbon dioxide gas from air pollution acts like a glass shield, retaining heat within the Earth's atmosphere.
2. The rate of temperature increase inside the jar is faster.

Think and Explore
Many governments require automobiles to pass an exhaust emission test every year. Find out how this testing can help to reduce the greenhouse effect.

How Can We Reduce the Risk of Radon Poisoning?

Background
Radon gas is produced by the natural breakdown of uranium, a radioactive substance found inside the Earth. Radon gas is colorless and odorless. It is harmful to health, causing such problems as lung cancer.

Materials
none needed

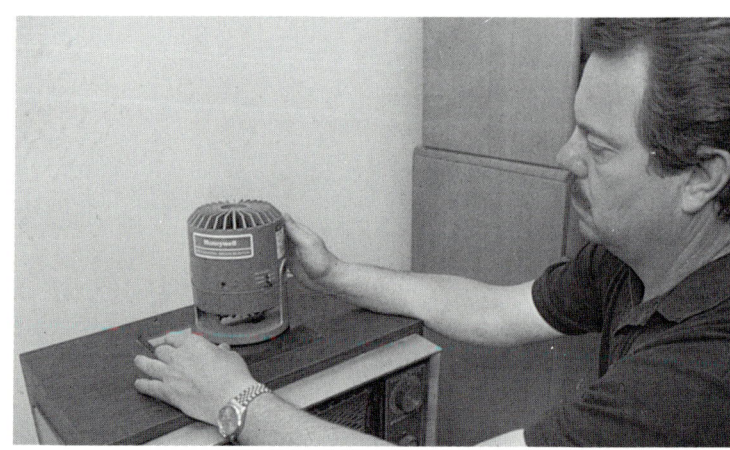

Procedure
1. Study the following scenario and diagram on page 63:
   A house was tested for radon gas. The results showed a high level of radon gas. The radon test consultant showed a cutaway view of the basement to the house owner.
2. How might the owner of the house eliminate or reduce the risk of radon poisoning? You might consider the following:
   (a) Based on the diagram, where are the possible radon entry points?
   (b) How would you stop the gas from entering the house?

Think and Explore
Consult your state Environmental Protection Agency (EPA) about possible radon problems in your area. Is your home safe from harmful radon gas?

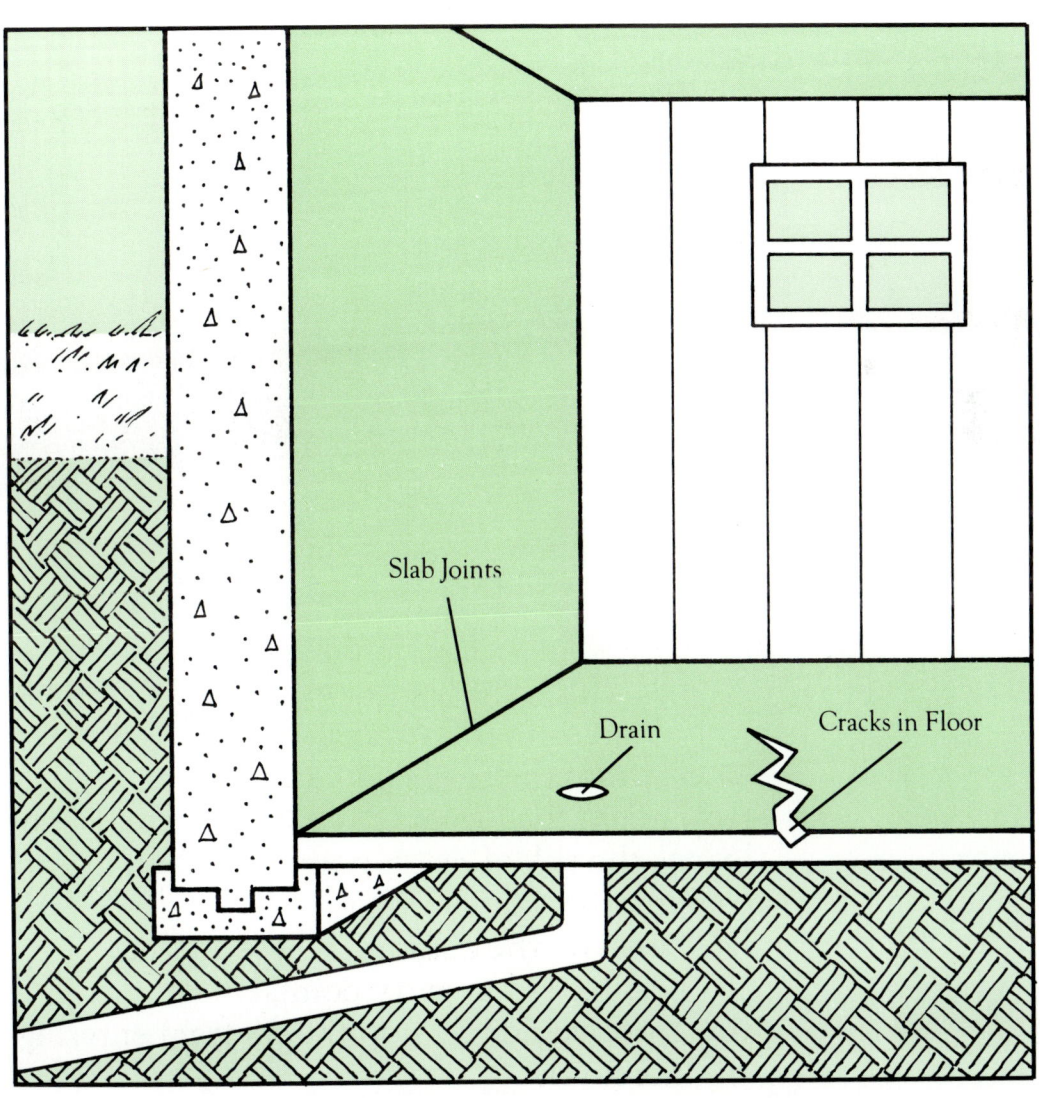

Chapter 3

Operation Clean Water

We tend to take water for granted. Water covers about 70 percent of the Earth's surface in oceans, lakes, rivers, and streams. About 97 percent of the Earth's water is in the oceans. Ocean water is too salty to be used for drinking, farming, and manufacturing. Only about 3 percent of the Earth's water is fresh (unsalty) water.

We cannot live without fresh water. Do you know that your body is about two-thirds water? You need to take in about 1 quart (0.9 liter) of water per day to replace water you lose naturally. Water is also vital for industry and agriculture in our modern-day society. Unfortunately, this important natural resource is very susceptible to all types of pollution. Mother Nature recycles and self-cleans water. But nature can only do so much! People dump more wastes such as oil and chemicals into water than nature can handle. There is no quick way to clean up the Earth's water—once it is polluted it stays that way for a long time. Our best hope is to avoid adding further pollution. We need clean water!

Is Your Drinking Water Free From Pollutants?

> NOTE: THIS ACTIVITY IS DIVIDED INTO PARTS A, B, AND C.

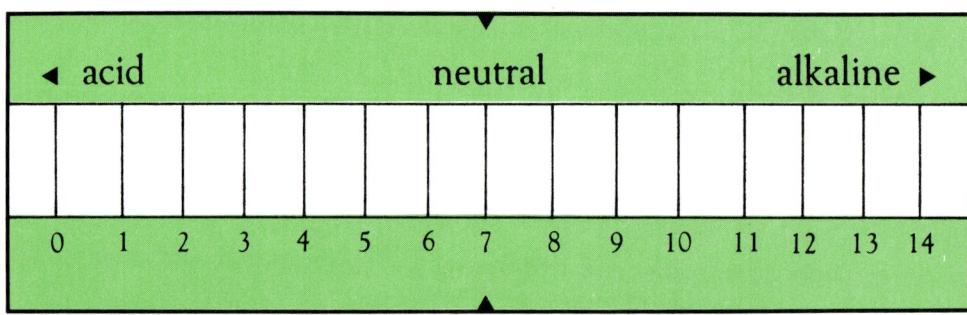

pH scale

Part A

What Is the pH of a Solution?

Materials
5 paper cups
lemon juice
water
grape juice
milk
baking soda
pH test paper (wide-range pH paper, with pH values from 2 to 10)
pH color chart
paper towel

> DO THIS ACTIVITY UNDER AN ADULT'S SUPERVISION

Procedure
1. Pour lemon juice, water, grape juice, baking soda water (dissolve baking soda in water), and milk into the five cups respectively. Label the cups.
2. Dip the pH test paper into each solution, take it out, and observe the color change. Record the data and compare the color to the pH color chart.
3. Can you arrange the solutions in order from the most acidic (pH between 0 and 7) to the most alkaline (pH between 7 and 14)? Which liquid is the most acidic? The most alkaline?

Conclusions
1. Acidity and alkalinity are special properties of solutions that can be measured by a pH scale. The pH scale goes from 0 (acid) to 14 (alkaline). Pure water falls in the middle of the scale at pH 7, or neutral. A higher pH value indicates that the material is more alkaline. A lower pH value indicates that the material is more acidic.
2. In the pH experiment, lemon juice is the most acidic, with a pH value of about 2.3. Baking soda solution is the most alkaline, with a pH value of about 9.

Think and Explore
1. Pure water has a pH value of 7. What does it mean if water has a pH value of 5.6?
2. Do you consider water with a pH value of 1 or 13 safe to consume? Can you explain?

Part B

What Is the pH of Rainwater?

Materials
polyethylene bag
tin can
stake
rubber bands
pH test paper
pH color chart

Procedure
1. Make a rain collector.
2. Put the rain collector in an open area away from buildings and overhanging trees.
3. Collect rainwater. (In winter, you can use melted snow.)
4. Pour the collected rainwater into a clean, dry paper cup.
5. Dip the pH test paper into the water, take it out, and observe any color change. Compare the paper to the pH color chart. What is the pH of the rainwater?

Conclusions
1. Rainwater is naturally slightly acidic because it contains a weak acid formed from the carbon dioxide gas in the air. The pH value of a weak acid should be between 6 and 7.
2. If your rainwater sample is in the pH 5 range — less than pH 6 — it is more than slightly acidic.

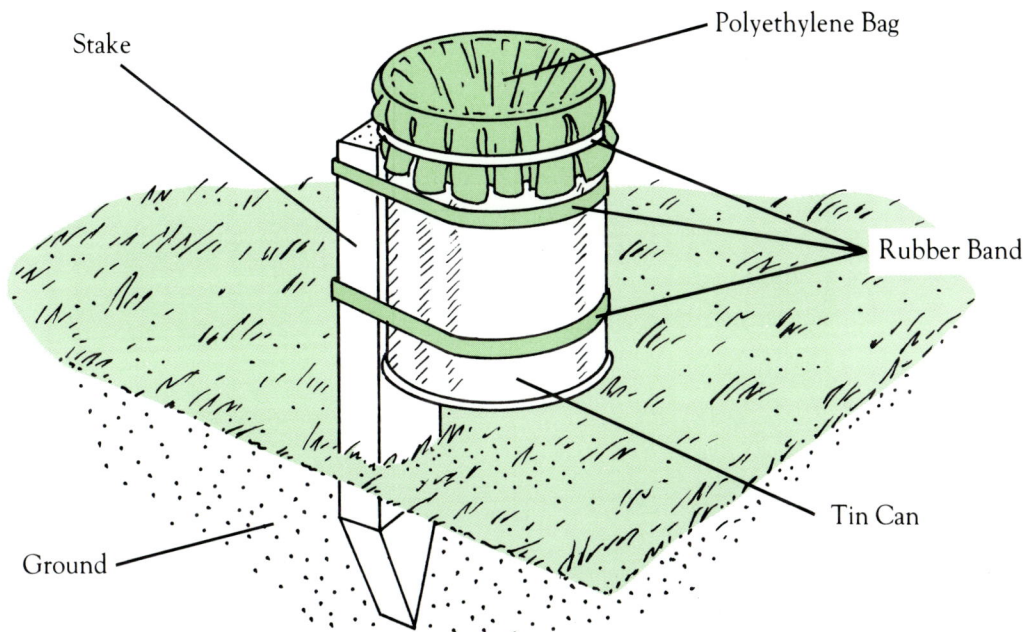

RAIN COLLECTOR

What might make the rainwater more acidic than normal?

Think and Explore

1. Acid Town is a community with many industries that burn coal and wood. The cities downwind of Acid Town are facing a serious problem—acid rain is damaging the forests and killing fish in the lakes and streams. Can you identify the source of the acid-rain problem? Why does the acid rain fall downwind from Acid Town?
2. Big cities on the east coast of the United States have serious acid-rain problems compared to cities in the Midwestern states. Can you explain why?
3. How do you propose to solve the acid-rain problem?

Part C

What Is the pH of Tap Water?

Materials
tap water
distilled water
2 paper cups
pH test paper
pH color chart

Procedure
1. Put tap water in one cup and distilled water in the other cup. Label the cups.
2. Dip a strip of the pH test paper into the cup with the tap water, take it out, and record the color change. Write down your data. Do the same for the cup with the distilled water.

Conclusions
1. Tap water varies in pH value depending on the community in which you live. Water from wells, water from lakes, and water from other sources will have different pH values.
2. Because of its method of preparation—distillation—distilled water should be very close to a pH value of 7, which is neutral.

Think and Explore
1. Which water supply, lake water or groundwater, is more likely to be polluted? Can you explain?
2. How could you compare the pH of the water in your community with that of a neighboring community's water? How do you find out?

How Do You Clean Water?

Materials
1 large plastic bottle (soft-drink bottle) with cap
plastic straw
cotton
large gravel
small gravel
large-grain sand
fine-grain sand
filter paper (larger than the diameter of the plastic bottle)
clean paper cup

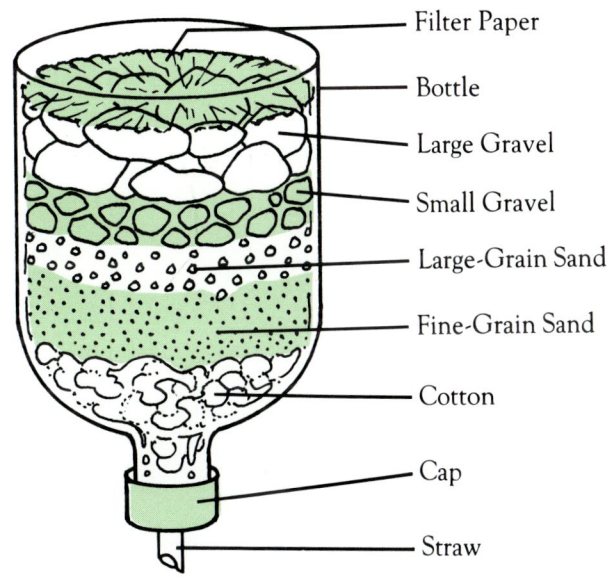

Procedure
1. Build a water filter according to the diagram. Cut out the bottom of the plastic bottle, turn the bottle upside down. Poke a hole in the lid of the bottle just large enough to fit the plastic straw. Put one end of the straw through the hole.
2. Pack the filtering materials—cotton, gravel, and sand—in layers from the narrow neck of the bottle to the open end.
3. Pour muddy water into the open top of the bottle and let the water seep down through the filter layers.
4. Collect the filtered water dripping from the straw. How does the filtered water differ from the muddy water you poured into the bottle.

Conclusion
The sand, gravel, and cotton layers filtered out the impurities in the muddy water. This cleaning process is similar to the filtering of air as described in the previous experiment.

A solid-waste storage area at the Oak Ridge National Laboratory in Oak Ridge, Tennessee

Think and Explore

1. Is the filtered muddy water safe to drink? Can you explain?
2. Natural spring water from the ground is known for its purity. Do you know why?
3. Sewage-treatment plants clean water by the action of bacteria. How does this differ from the process used in a water-filtering plant?
4. Under the Safe Drinking Water Act, the U.S. Environmental Protection Agency (EPA) sets national standards to protect drinking water. Write to your state EPA to find out about these standards. (You will find the address in the Yellow Pages.)

How Does an Ocean Oil Spill Affect Wildlife?

NOTE: THIS ACTIVITY IS DIVIDED INTO PARTS A AND B.

Part A

What Is the Effect of an Oil Spill on Eggs?

Materials

cooking oil (dirty motor oil is preferred if it is available)
shallow aluminum pie pan
medicine dropper
3 hard-boiled eggs

Procedure

1. Fill a shallow aluminum pie pan with water. Use the medicine dropper to add enough oil to the water to simulate water pollution by an ocean oil spill.
2. Add three unshelled, hard-boiled eggs to the water.
3. Remove one egg after five minutes. Peel off the shell and examine the egg. Remove and examine the second egg after 15 minutes, and the third egg after 30 minutes.
4. Record your observations.

Think and Explore
What effect could oil have on the eggs of birds nesting on beaches near water that has been polluted by an oil spill?

Part B

What Is the Effect of an Oil Spill on Feathers?

Materials
cooking oil (dirty motor oil is preferred if it is available)
a natural bird feather
medicine dropper
magnifier

Procedure
1. Examine a natural bird feather with a magnifier.
2. Dip the feather into water for one minute, take it out, and examine it with a magnifier.
3. Dip the clean feather into oil for one minute, take it out, and examine it with a magnifier.
4. Now dip the oil-covered feather in the water for one minute. Examine the feather with the magnifier.
5. Compare your observations in steps 1, 2, 3, and 4. What are the major changes in the clean feather after exposure to plain water? To oil? What are the changes when the oil-covered feather is dipped in water?

Conclusion
A natural feather has the ability to repel water, and this ability is affected by exposure to oil.

Think and Explore
1. How does exposure to oil affect normal bird activities?
2. How would you propose to rescue birds that have been exposed to an oil spill?
3. What are other examples of human-caused pollutants that can have harmful effects on wildlife?
4. Find out the water-quality standards set by your state in compliance with the Clean Water Act.

Chapter 4

Operation Clean Land

People produce trash, sometimes called solid waste. These wastes are thrown away because they are not wanted, no longer useful, harmful, or unpleasant to keep. About 3½ pounds (1.5 kilograms) of solid waste is thrown away every day by each person in the United States—a total of 1 billion pounds (0.4 billion kilograms) of garbage per day. What happens to trash after it is taken away from your home? Most of it is dumped in landfills—large holes in the ground. In sanitary landfills, the trash is covered with a layer of soil to prevent the decaying garbage from polluting the air. Today, there are probably more than twenty thousand landfills in the United States. Landfills are hazardous to the environment as well as to our health and they take up more and more space. Worst of all, decomposed garbage pollutes the soil and the groundwater supply. Clean land is a limited and precious resource. We need to protect it!

What Is a Landfill and Why Are Landfills Becoming a Problem?

Materials
tall glass jar
plastic fork
potting soil
piece of fruit
aluminum foil
toilet paper
plastic foam cup

Procedure
1. Create a miniature landfill. Put some soil in the bottom of a tall glass jar. Place small pieces of a plastic fork, fruit, aluminum foil, toilet paper, and a plastic foam cup in the jar, separated by thin layers of soil. Place the materials against the side of the jar so that you can see them through the glass.
2. Cover the top with another layer of soil.
3. Record your observations every week for several weeks. What is happening to the plastic? Fruit? Aluminum foil? Paper? Plastic foam? Do they come apart or decompose in the soil?

Conclusion
Trash is made of many materials. Some trash materials are degradable (able to decompose); others last for a long time; some may last forever!

Think and Explore

1. Why are landfills hazardous to the environment?
2. How do sanitary landfills reduce the risk of pollution?
3. Most landfills today are designed to be used for about 20 years. What can people do with the land after the landfill is filled and closed? Would you recommend that the land be used for parks, office buildings, parking lots, or schools? Can you explain?
4. Find out from your state Environmental Protection Agency (EPA) the standards for landfills that are used to dispose of hazardous wastes.

How Can Some Substances Be Toxic to Living Things?

Materials
2 paper cups
2 bean seeds
potting soil
salt
water

Procedure
1. Fill each cup to about 1/2 inch (1.2 centimeters) from the top with potting soil. Label one cup A and the other B.
2. Plant a bean seed in each cup. Put the cups in a sunny spot and water both cups regularly until the seeds sprout and you have two small bean plants. (The soil should remain moist, but do not overwater.)
3. Water Plant A with ordinary tap water. Water Plant B with tap water mixed with about a teaspoon of salt.
4. Record your observations of each plant after a few days.

Conclusion
Certain chemicals, such as salt, can be harmful to living things. These harmful substances may leak from landfills where trash is decomposing.

Think and Explore
Some of the decomposed trash in a landfill turns into a combustible natural gas called methane. This gas forms pockets in the landfill and can be dangerous unless it is removed. Suggest a plan to reduce the risk of a methane explosion. (HINT: Find out how methane gas can be used by people.)

What Are a Farmer's Alternatives to Using Toxic Chemicals?

Materials
3 paper cups
3 clear plastic cups
bean seeds
soil
pea aphids
lady bugs
pesticide for aphids

Procedure
1. Fill three paper cups with some soil. Label the cups A, B, and C.
2. Start a bean plant in each cup. Put the cups in a sunny spot and water them regularly.
3. Put some pea aphids on each bean plant and cover the plant with a perforated, clear-plastic cup. The plastic cups prevent the aphids from escaping, and the perforations allow the plant and the aphids to breathe. Aphids are pests that feed on plants. If they are not removed, they will kill the plant in a short time.
4. Introduce some ladybugs to cup A. Spray cup B with the insecticide. Do absolutely nothing with cup C.
5. Record your observations of cups A, B, and C. What happened to the bean plant in each cup?

> **DO THIS ACTIVITY UNDER AN ADULT'S SUPERVISION**

Conclusion

The aphids are killed by the ladybugs in cup A. The plant is not damaged because the ladybugs do not feed on the plant. The aphids are also killed by the pesticide in cup B; however, the plant and the soil are likely to be contaminated by the toxic chemical. The aphids in cup C will destroy the plant.

Think and Explore

1. Why is the use of natural predators, known as biological controls, to eliminate pests a good alternative to the use of the toxic chemicals found in pesticides? Can you name a few natural predators?
2. According to the standards set by the U.S. Environmental Protection Agency (EPA), dioxin, polychlorinated biphenyls (PCBs), ethylene dibromide (EDB), and asbestos are all on the "hit list" of toxic chemicals. Find out which one is more likely to pollute soil and land and affect the well-being of people.

Chapter 5

Save the Earth: Recycle

People have always had trash. Cave people did not have a big problem with it. In those days, there was plenty of room for dumping trash, and nature easily disposed of it. Today, however, trash is a big problem. More people produce more trash. Every year, on the average, each one of us throws away nearly 1 ton (0.9 metric ton) of trash. To get rid of it, people have burned it, but unfortunately, burning trash can cause air pollution. People have dumped it in the ocean. Unfortunately, this can pollute the ocean water. People have buried trash in landfills. But we are running out of empty land. Some people have even suggested shooting trash into outer space. But who wants old tennis shoes, rusty cans, and used newspaper going around the Earth?

In past years, people have found an effective way to get rid of some of our trash. It is called recycling. Recycling means reusing trash instead of getting rid of it. In recycling old cans and cars, metals are shredded and melted to make materials for new cans and cars. Glass bottles can be crushed into tiny glass bits and melted to make new glass. Recycling solves some of the problems of trash disposal. It also helps us to save natural resources by using the same materials over and over again. Old cans, plastics, and bottles can have more than just one life to live.

How Can Paper Be Recycled?

Materials
old newspaper
large bowl
blender (or an egg beater)
laundry starch
piece of window screening
plastic sheet
wood block

Procedure
1. Fill a large bowl ¼ full of water. Tear an old newspaper into small pieces and soak them overnight in the bowl.
2. Put the paper mixture in a blender and blend it to a creamy mixture. (An egg beater can be used, but it will take more work and time.) Pour the blended mixture back into the bowl.
3. Prepare a starch solution by dissolving 2 tablespoons of laundry starch in a pint of water. Add the solution to the bowl. Mix well.
4. Cut a round piece of screen smaller than the diameter of the bowl. Dip the screen into the blended mixture until a fairly thick layer of fibers accumulates on the screen.
5. Place the screen over a used newspaper. Cover the fibers with a plastic sheet and squeeze the water out with a wood block.

> **DO THIS ACTIVITY UNDER AN ADULT'S SUPERVISION**

6. Dry the fibers overnight. What will you get? Recycled paper!

Conclusion
Used paper can be recycled into usable materials.

Think and Explore
What benefits can we get from recycling used paper? (Hint: Paper is made from wood fibers.)

What Can Be Recycled and What Cannot?

Materials
none needed

Procedure
1. Visit a fast-food restaurant and order a meal.
2. Collect and save all the wrappers, cups, bags, straws, cutlery, napkins, and other things (not food) that you would throw away after the meal. Classify all the trash to see which items can be recycled and which cannot. Record your data.
3. Visit several other fast-food restaurants on different days and order a similar meal. Classify all the trash as you did before. Record your data.
4. Compare your trash data to see which fast-food restaurant used the most materials that cannot be recycled.

Conclusion
For the sake of convenience, fast-food restaurants in general create a lot of trash. Unfortunately, most of the trash, such as plastic and plastic foam, cannot be recycled.

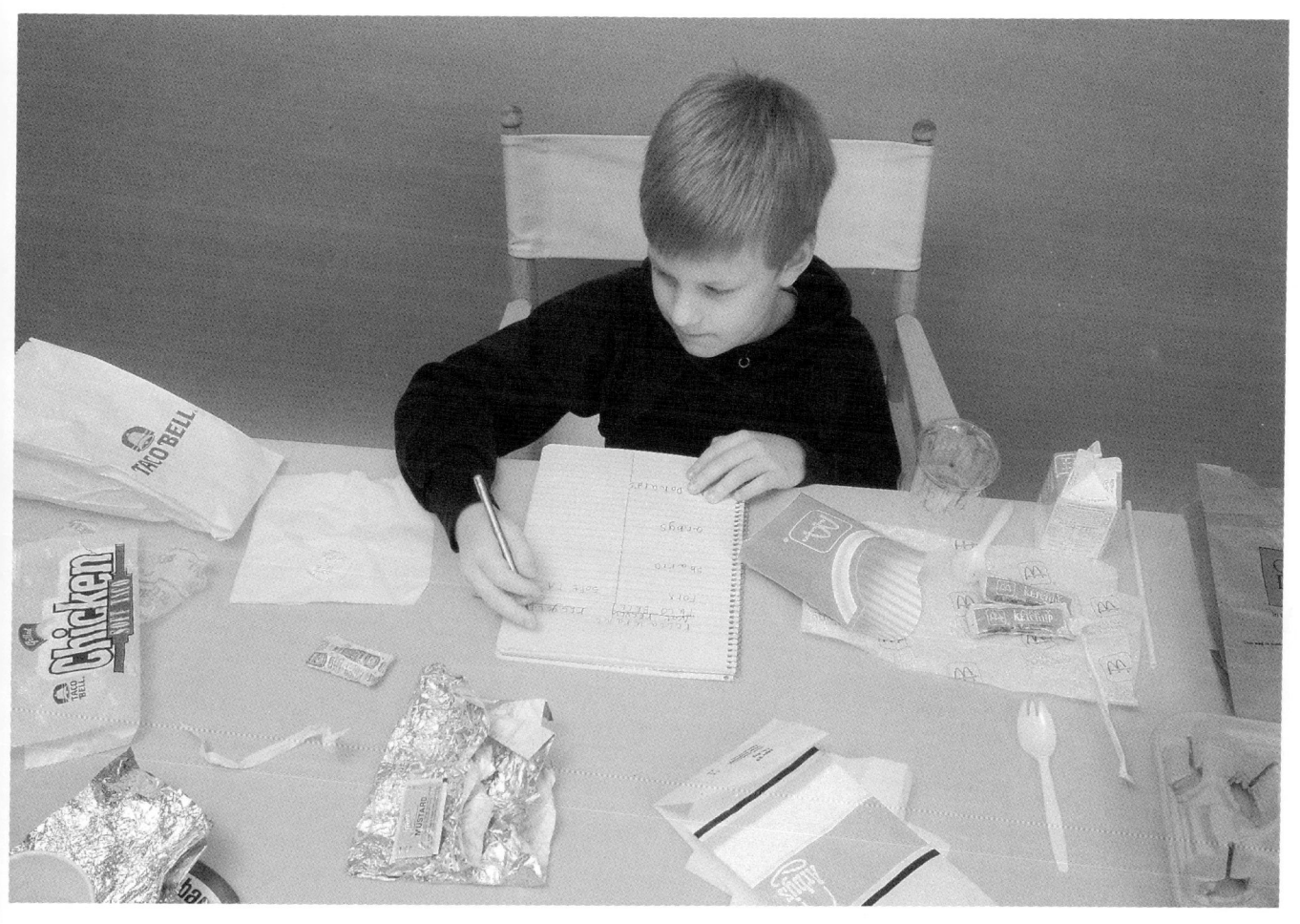

Think and Explore
1. Will refusing to eat at fast-food restaurants help us to reduce the amount of trash in landfills? Can you explain?
2. How would you advise fast-food restaurants to take steps toward saving our environment?

Chapter 6

Save the Earth: Conserve and Use Clean Energy

The United States has only about 6 percent of the world's population, but it uses close to 50 percent of the world's supply of energy. As the standard of living around the world rises, so will the demand for energy. When you turn on the television or turn up the heat in your home, you use energy—gas, oil, or electricity. When you eat a hot dog, you benefit from the farmers who raised the beef cattle and from the industries that made the meat packaging. But, do you realize that the process of cooking the hot dog, raising the cattle, and packaging the meat all demand the use of energy? The way that people use energy can either help keep our environment clean or make it dirty. Most of our energy comes from the burning of fossil fuels such as coal and oil, but these energy sources cause air pollution.

There are alternative sources of energy that do not pollute. Welcome to the tomorrow of using these sources of nonpolluting energy.

What Kind of Energy User Are You?

Materials
none needed

Procedure
1. Study the energy-use chart on page 101 carefully. Each energy use is given a score. Check only those items that are applicable to you.
2. Add up the total score for all the items that you checked.

Energy-use chart

Transportation to school	Score
(a) walk	1
(b) bicycle	2
(c) school bus	3
(d) car	4
Comfort (summertime)	**Score**
(e) window fan	1
(f) dehumidifier	2
(g) air conditioner	3
Entertainment	**Score**
(h) radio	1
(i) television (black & white)	2
(j) television (color)	3
Kitchen appliances	**Score**
(k) refrigerator	1
(l) blender	2
(m) dishwasher	3
(n) microwave oven	4

total score _____

3. What is your total score? Under 10? 11 to 20? Above 20?

Conclusions

Your daily activities can classify you as an energy user under the following categories: necessity, convenience, or luxury.

If you score below 10, then you are a necessity energy user. A necessity is something you would have a hard time living without.

If you score from 11 to 20, you are a convenience energy user. A convenience is something that makes life more pleasant or easier.

If you score above 20, you are a luxury energy user. A luxury is something that is not needed for everyday life.

Think and Explore

1. Can you suggest ways that you might use less energy in your daily activities?
2. How can energy conservation help to save the Earth's environment?

How Can You Conserve Energy in Your Home?

Materials
none needed

Procedure
1. Ask an adult for a gas or electric bill. Find out the amount of the bill.
2. Discuss the following checklist with your parents and use it to change or modify the energy-use activities in your home as much as possible. Keep up the changes or modifications until the next billing period.
3. Do you see savings in the gas or electric bill? How can the change be related to your energy conservation measures?

Energy Conservation Checklist

(a) Set the refrigerator at 40 degrees Fahrenheit (F.) or 4 degrees Celsius (C).
(b) Use the washer and dryer only for full loads.
(c) Dry clothes on a clothesline in clear and sunny weather.
(d) Take quick showers instead of baths.
(e) Close windows and doors when heating or air-conditioning systems are on.
(f) In winter, set the furnace thermostat at 70° F. (21°C).
(g) Use the dishwasher only when it is full.
(h) Close off vents and doors to empty rooms when you are using the air-cooling or heating system.
(i) Turn off lights and electric appliances when they are not in use.

Conclusion

These are ways that energy may be conserved in the home. If you conserve energy, you are using less of the Earth's natural resources that produce the energy.

Think and Explore

1. Which of the following is the biggest energy user in the home—water heater, refrigerator, television, range? How can you find out?
2. A watt is a unit for measuring how much electric energy is being used. Find out the average wattage of an electric clock, a vacuum cleaner, a hair dryer, an iron, and a coffee maker. (Hint: Find the information in the operating manual for the appliance.)

What Is Solar Energy?

Materials
a magnifier
3 sheets of construction paper
   (white, gray, and black)
watch

Procedure
1. Position a magnifier on a bright sunny day so that the sun's rays are focused on a piece of white construction paper. What happens? The paper chars and eventually catches fire!
2. Repeat step one again, and time it. How long does it take the white paper to char? The gray paper? The black paper?
3. Record your data in the following table:

Paper	Time to char (seconds)
white	_____
gray	_____
black	_____

4. Which color paper takes the shortest time to char? The longest time?

DO THIS ACTIVITY UNDER AN ADULT'S SUPERVISION

Conclusions
1. The sun's energy (solar energy) produces both light and heat.
2. The sun's energy can be harvested to do work. In the experiment, the magnifier is a tool to collect and focus the sun's rays to raise the temperature high enough to char the paper.

Think and Explore
1. How can the sun be used wisely as an alternative clean source of energy?
2. The GM Sun Raycer is a solar-powered car. How does the car run on a cloudy day when the sun is hardly visible?

What Is Solar Distillation?

Materials
muddy water
2-pound (0.9 kilogram) coffee can
plastic wrap
small drinking cup
small pebble
rubber band

Procedure
1. Put about 2 inches (5 centimeters) of muddy water in the coffee can.
2. Place a small drinking cup in the middle of the can
3. Cover the opening of the can with plastic wrap and secure the wrap with a rubber band around the can.
4. Place a small pebble in the center of the wrap so that the wrap sags toward the middle.
5. Put the setup in the bright sunlight for a few hours and record your observations.

Conclusion
Clean water will be collected very slowly in the cup by solar distillation. Water is being evaporated by the heat from the sun. The vapor condenses on the plastic wrap and drips into the drinking cup. People in the desert sometimes use solar distillation to get clean drinking water.

109

Think and Explore
1. What happens to the impurities (the mud) as the water is being distilled?
2. Why do some people use bottled drinking water instead of tap water?
3. After a shipwreck, Tom is stranded in a small boat on the ocean. He runs out of drinking water. Can you suggest a way for him to get drinking water? (Hint: What is desalinization?)

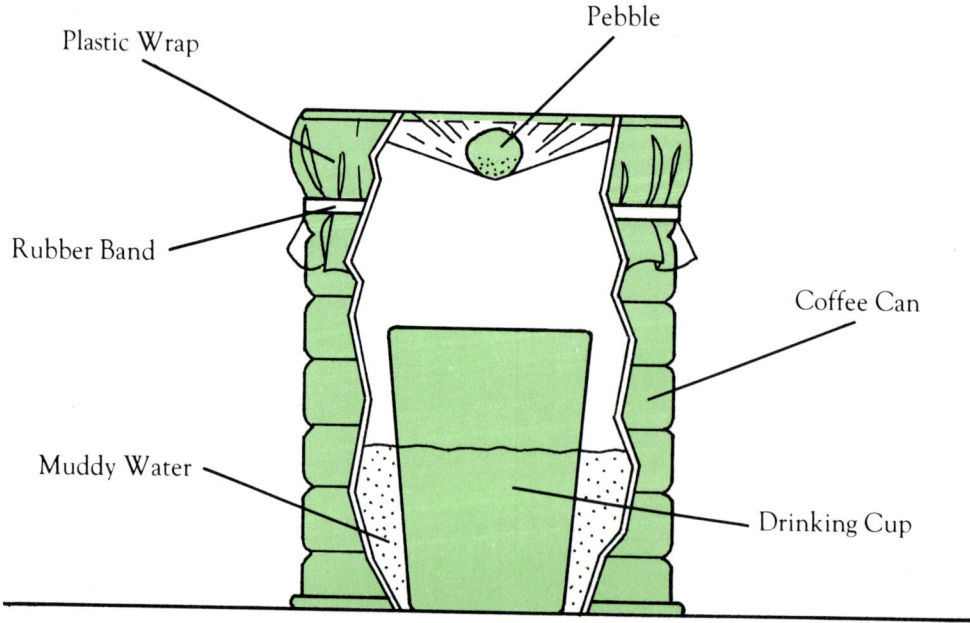

How Can You Heat Water With Solar Energy?

Materials
2 aluminum pie pans
plastic wrap
thermometer
black paint

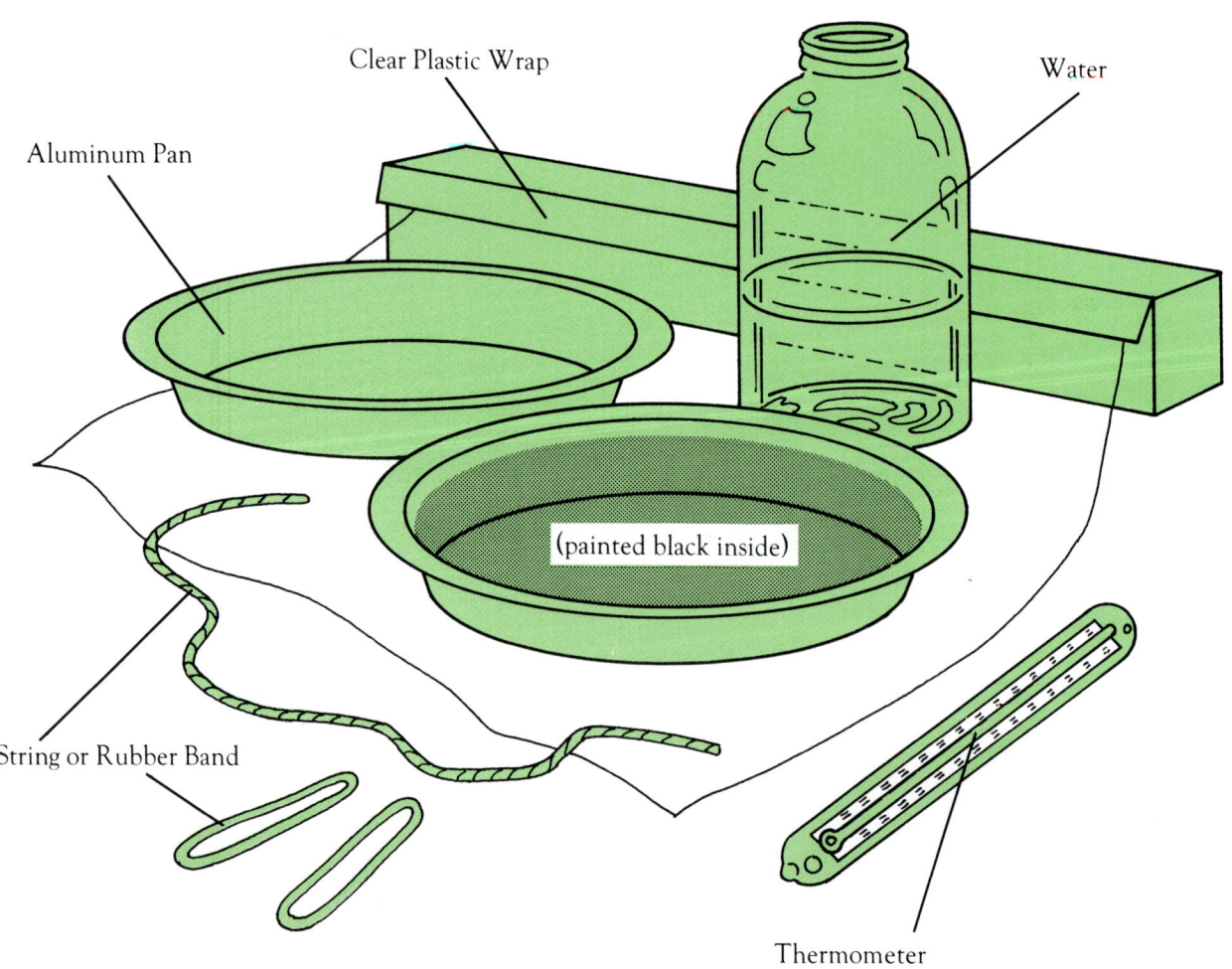

Procedure
1. Paint the inside of one aluminum pie pan black. Leave the other pan unpainted.
2. Pour some water in both pans. Make sure that the same amount of water is put in both pans.
3. Put a thermometer in each pan and cover both pans with clear plastic wrap. The wrap can be secured by tying a string around the pan or by using a rubber band.
4. Put both pans in a bright, sunny area.
5. Make a chart like the following and record the rise in water temperature for each pan every 2 minutes.

Time (min.)	Black Pan (°F.) (°C)	Unpainted Pan (°F.) (°C)
start	_____	_____
2	_____	_____
4	_____	_____
6	_____	_____
8	_____	_____
10	_____	_____
12	_____	_____
14	_____	_____
16	_____	_____

6. Compare the temperature rise in the pans. Which one converts more solar energy into heat?

Conclusion
Dark colors absorb heat faster than light colors.
A dark color converts more solar energy to heat.

Think and Explore
1. Repeat the experiment using two unpainted pans. Add enough ink or food coloring to one pan to make the water very dark. Which pan do you think will produce more heat from the sun?
2. Have you seen a flat-plate solar collector on the roof of a house? Find out how hot water is produced and circulated in a solar water-heating system.

Chapter 7

Action: Putting It All Together

There are two things that are permanent in this country, two things that we pass on from generation to generation, without even speaking of our pride or their preciousness. One is the treasure of the mind and hearts. The other is the treasure of our land—the environment.
—President George Bush

Do you think you and your friends can save our environment from destruction? You can say, "I do not know," or you can say, "Yes, I do!" If you think that one or two people cannot possibly make a difference in saving the environment because you do not have the power to do it, you are wrong! If you are serious about saving the environment, our planet Earth, then what you believe, say, and do will make an impact on other people. Remember, there is a ripple effect in all that we do. What you do touches other people, and it goes on, and on, and on . . . .

Have You Hugged Your Planet Today?

Materials
none needed

Procedure
1. Study the following action plan carefully and take action on things that you can do to save the environment.
2. How many of the following can you do?

(A) Save the Air
   1. Plant a tree. Trees produce oxygen, which is needed for a healthy environment.
   2. Walk or ride a bike for short trips. Car exhaust pollutes the air.
   3. Identify sources of air pollution in your community. Write to local authorities to tell them that you are concerned about air pollution.

(B) Save the Water
   1. Repair leaky faucets and stop water wastage. Conserve water whenever and wherever possible.
   2. Turn off the water when you brush your teeth or when you put soap on your hands.
   3. Take quick showers instead of baths. You use less water in the shower than in a bath.
   4. Do not dump harmful liquids onto the ground. The liquids can seep into the ground and contaminate the groundwater.

5. Identify sources of water pollution in your community. Write to local authorities to tell them that you are concerned about water pollution.

(C) Save the Trees
1. Bring a bag with you when you go shopping. Paper bags are made from wood fibers. When you save a paper bag, you also save a tree!
2. Write on both sides of a piece of paper. When you save paper, you save trees.
3. Use an artificial Christmas tree and stop buying cut trees. Do you know how long it takes to grow a 5-foot (1.5-meter) Christmas tree?

(D) Use Energy Wisely
 1. Turn off lights and appliances when they are not in use. Remember, the energy you use comes from the Earth's resources.
 2. Use daylight as much as possible. It is free and it is clean. If you can use sunlight near a window to read a book, do it.
 3. Adjust your clothing instead of adjusting the thermostat.
 4. Rinse clean dishes with cold water. Conserving hot water saves both water and energy!
 5. Close doors and windows when the heating or cooling system is on.
 6. Do not open the refrigerator unless you have to. It takes energy to keep the refrigerator cool.
 7. Cover a pot when you are boiling water. It takes more energy to boil a pot of water without a lid.

(E) Recycle
 1. Recycle glass bottles, used newspaper, metal cans, and plastic milk bottles.

Recycling saves both natural resources and energy.
2. Stop the use of nondegradable materials such as plastic-foam products. Any nondegradable product pollutes our environment.

(F) Spread the Word
1. Share what you have learned with family and friends.
2. Organize environmental-awareness meetings at home and at school to promote things that all of us can do to save the Earth.

Conclusion

You do not have to be a grown-up to help save the environment. You can help if you care about the future of the Earth.

Think and Explore

1. Can you extend the list of what you can do to save the environment?
2. What are some of the things that only grown-ups can do to save the environment? Can you explain?
3. People can do many things to save our environment. We can stop pollution. We can increase the budget for environmental protection. We can stop population growth. We can put ecology in the school curriculum. What do you think is the single most important thing that people can do? Can you explain why you think so?

WORDS YOU SHOULD KNOW

ACID RAIN — Rain that has the properties of an acid. Pollutants such as sulfur dioxide gas from the burning of fossil fuels dissolve in water in the air. The water falls as acid rain or snow.

BIOLOGICAL CONTROL — The use of an organism to control the population of another organism. The controlling organism preys on the organism to be controlled.

CARBON DIOXIDE — A colorless gas that is released naturally through the respiration of living things. Carbon dioxide makes up about 0.03 percent of the air.

CARRYING CAPACITY — The number of organisms that an environment can support. The availability of natural resources such as food and water usually affects the carrying capacity of the environment.

CONSERVATION — The saving of the natural resources of the Earth from destruction.

DEGRADABLE MATERIALS — Materials that can be decomposed naturally by the action of bacteria.

DISTILLATION — A method of separating unwanted materials from a liquid. The liquid is heated until it evaporates, and the unwanted materials are left behind.

ECOLOGY — The study of living things in relation to their surroundings.

ENDANGERED — In danger of dying out completely.

ENERGY — The ability to do work; things used to do work, such as fuels.

ENVIRONMENT — The things that surround a living thing, including the air, water, and land.

EXTINCT — No longer living. Extinct species have completely died out.

FOOD CHAIN — A linear arrangement of the organisms in a community in the order in which each organism uses the next lower member as a source of food.

FOSSIL FUEL — Materials that consist of the remains of plants or animals that lived long ago and that are burned to produce energy.

GREENHOUSE EFFECT — The warming of the Earth's atmosphere produced by the overaccumulation of carbon dioxide gas. Carbon dioxide acts as a shield to keep the heat in, much like a greenhouse.

INDICATOR — A chemical that changes color in the presence of another substance.

LANDFILL — A place where solid waste is dumped or buried.

METHANE — A gas produced by the action of bacteria on decaying plant and animal remains.

NATURAL RESOURCES — All the things in the world that are used by living things. Air, food, and water are natural resources.

OXYGEN — A gas that supports life. It makes up nearly 21 percent of the air.

pH — A scale for measuring acidity and alkalinity. The pH scale goes from 1 to 14. A pH value from 1 to 6.9 indicates acid. A pH value from 7.1 to 14 indicates alkaline. A pH value of 7 is neutral.

POLLUTION — The addition of harmful substances to the air, water, or soil.

RADON — A harmful gas produced by the natural breakdown of uranium.

RECYCLING — Using things such as paper, glass, and metals over and over again.

SMOG — A form of air pollution. It is a haze in the air caused by the action of sunlight on air pollutants and water vapor.

Index

acidity, **67, 68, 69**
acid rain, **9, 69**. *See also* water pollution.
agriculture, **9**
   insecticides and, **88-89**
air, **11, 12, 14, 22, 24, 35, 44**. *See also* air pollution.
   animals and, **44**
   carbon dioxide in, **44, 61**
   plants and, **44, 118**
air pollution, **9, 49, 80, 118**
   automobile exhausts and, **46, 61, 118**
   burning and, **46, 69, 91, 98**
   carbon dioxide gas and, **61**
   cigarette smoke and, **56-58**
   experiments with, **47-49, 50-52, 54-55, 56-58, 60-61**
   factories and, **46**
   filters and, **54-55**
   fossil fuels and, **46**
   living things and, **46, 52**
   radon gas and, **62-63**
   spray cans and, **46**
   weather conditions and, **49**
alkalinity, **67**
animals, **17, 24**. *See also* populations; tracks, animal.
   carbon dioxide gas and, **38-39, 42-43**
   extinct or endangered, **32-35**
   groups of, **33**
   as predators, **26, 27, 89**
   as prey, **26, 27, 89**
aphids, **88**
asbestos, **89**
astronauts, **12**
atmosphere, **44, 46**. *See also* air.
automobiles
   air filters in, **55**
   emission tests, **61**
   exhausts, **46, 61**
bacteria, sewage treatment and, **75**

bald eagle, **35**
biological controls, **89**
blue whale, **35**
bottles, recycling, **91, 120**
bromothymol blue (BTB) solution, **36, 37, 38, 39, 40-41, 42**
building materials, **30**
cans, recycling, **91, 120**
carbon dioxide gas
   animals and, **38-39, 42-43**
   breathing and, **39**
   chemical indicator and, **36-37**
   experiment with, **36-43**
   greenhouse effect and, **61**
   plants and, **40-41, 42-43**
   rainwater and, **68**
carbonic acid, **37, 39**
catalytic converter, **55**
chemicals, toxic, **85, 86, 87, 118**
   farmers and, **88-89**
Christmas trees, **119**
cigarettes, disease and, **58**
Clean Air Act, **55**
Clean Water Act, **79**
coal, energy from, **98**
dinosaurs, **35**
dioxin, **89**
ecologists, **11**
electricity, **98**
   use of, in home, **104-105**
endangered species. *See* animals, extinct or endangered.
energy
   alternative sources of, **98, 106-107, 108-110**
   conservation of, **102, 104-105, 120**
   experiments with, **100-115**
   fossil fuels and, **98**
   solar, **106-107, 108-110, 112-115**
   use of, **100-102, 104-105**

energy-use chart, **100, 101**
environment
   basic needs of life and, **17, 24**
   carrying capacity of, **22, 24, 25**
   carbon dioxide gas in, **42-43**
   energy use and, **98, 102**
   extinction and, **35**
   interdependence of living things with, **11, 36-43**
   pollution of, **9, 80, 83.** *See also* air pollution; soil pollution; water pollution.
   experiments with saving, **118-121**
   wildlife interacting with, **18, 20, 27**
Environmental Protection Agency (EPA), **55, 63, 75, 83, 89**
ethylene dibromide (EDB), **89**
factories, **46**
fast-food restaurants, trash and, **96**
filters
   air, **54, 55**
   water, **73, 74, 75**
fish and fisheries, **9, 69**
food, **11, 12, 14, 20, 22, 24, 30**
food chain, **27**
forests, **69**
forest fires, **46**
forest preserves, **18**
fruit flies
   culture, **22, 24**
   experiment with, **22, 24-25**
   population of, **22, 24, 25**
garbage. *See also* trash.
   burning of, **46**
gas, natural
   energy from, **98**
   use of, in home, **104**
gaseous exchange, cycle of, **43**
GM Sun Raycer, **107**
greenhouse effect, **60-61**
groundwater, **71, 75, 80, 118**

hornwort, **41, 42, 43**
hunting, **35**
insecticide, **88, 89**
ladybugs, **88, 89**
lakes, **18, 69**
   drinking water from, **71**
land, pollution of. *See* soil pollution.
landfills, **80, 82, 86, 87, 91, 97**
methane gas, **87**
needs of life, basic, **11, 12, 14, 22, 24**
   availability of, **15**
   game about, **15-16**
   populations and, **15-17**
oceans, **65, 91**
oil, energy from, **98**
oil spills, **9**
   birds' eggs and, **76-77**
   birds' feathers and, **78-79**
owl pellets, **26, 27, 29**
owls, **26, 27, 29**
pandas, **35**
paper, **95, 119**
pesticide. *See* insecticide.
pH. *See also* pH scale.
   color chart, **67, 68, 70**
   of drinking water, **66-67**
   of rainwater, **68-69**
   of tap water, **70-71**
   test paper and, **66-67, 68-69, 70-71**
pH scale, **67, 68**
plants, **24.** *See also* trees.
   carbon dioxide gas and, **40-41**
   human needs and, **30-31**
   pests and, **88-89**
plaster cast, **18, 20**
plaster of paris, **20**
plastic, **91, 96, 120**
plastic foam, **96, 121**
pollution. *See* air pollution; soil pollution; water pollution.

polychlorinated biphenyls (PCBs), **89**
populations
    animal, **17**
    basic needs of life and, **15-17, 22, 24**
    of fruit flies, **22, 24, 25**
    human, **25**
    record of, **22, 24**
radon gas, **62-63**
    basements and, **62-63**
    disease and, **62**
recycling
    cans, **91**
    experiments with, **92-97**
    fast-food restaurants and, **96-97**
    glass, **91, 120**
    metals, **91, 120**
    paper, **92-95, 120**
    plastics, **91, 120**
resources, **14**
    conserving, **12, 14, 105**
    natural, **9, 30, 105**
Safe Drinking Water Act, **75**
salt toxic to plants, **85-86**
sewage-treatment plants, **75**
snails, **38, 39, 42, 43**
soil pollution
    experiments with, **82-89**
    hazardous wastes and, **83**
    landfills and, **82, 83, 85, 86**
solar energy. *See* energy; sun, energy from.
solid waste. *See* trash.
space, **11, 22, 24, 35**
spaceship, **12, 14**
spray cans, **46**
streams, **18, 20, 69**
sun, **44**
    energy from, **106-107, 108, 110, 112-115**
    solar distillation and, **108-110**
tourism, **9**

toxic chemicals. *See* chemicals, toxic.
tracks, animal, **18, 20**
trash, **80, 91**. *See also* chemicals, toxic; recycling.
    degradable, **82, 121**
    fast-food restaurants and, **96-97**
    landfills and, **80, 82, 83, 86, 87**
trees, **31, 119**
    environment and, **31, 43, 118**
    oxygen and, **118**
    paper from, **95, 119**
uranium, radon gas and, **62**
wastes. *See* trash.
water, **11, 12, 14, 20, 22, 24, 35, 37, 44**. *See also* groundwater; water pollution.
    agriculture and, **65**
    cleaning, **72, 73, 74, 75**
    conserving, **118**
    drinking, **66-67, 71, 75, 108, 110**
    distilled, **71, 108, 110**
    filtering, **73, 74, 75**
    fresh, **65**
    heating, with solar energy, **112-115**
    industry and, **65**
    in oceans, **65**
    solar distillation and, **108-110**
    sources of, **71**
water pollution, **9, 65, 118, 119**
    drinking water and, **66-67, 75**
    experiments with, **66-79**
    landfills and, **80**
    oil spills and, **9, 76-79**
    rainwater and, **68-69**
    trash and, **91**
    wildlife and, **76-79**
watts, **105**
weather, **44, 49**
wells, water from, **71**
wood bison, **35**
wood fibers, paper and, **95, 119**
World Wildlife Fund, **35**

About the author

Ovid K. Wong earned his B.Sc. in biology from the University of Alberta, Edmonton, Canada; his M.Ed. in curriculum from the University of Washington, Seattle; and his Ph.D. in science education from the University of Illinois, Urbana-Champaign. He is currently the principal of W. A. Johnson School in Bensenville, Illinois. Since 1984 he has served as a consultant for the Illinois State Board of Education and the State Board of Higher Education.

Dr. Wong's work has appeared on public television and in such journals as the *Science Teacher*, the *American Biology Teacher*, *ISTA Spectrum*, the *Bilingual Journal*, the *Illinois Principals*, and a number of professional newsletters. He is the author of *Giant Pandas*, *Prehistoric People*, *Experiments with Animal Behavior*, *Your Body and How It Works*, and *Is Science Magic?* from Childrens Press, and has written a Glossary of Biology for Greenwood Press.

In 1989, Dr. Wong was named Outstanding Science Teacher in Illinois by the National Science Foundation. He also received the 1989 Science Teaching Achievement Recognition (STAR) award from the National Science Teachers Association. Dr. Wong is listed in the 1989-1990 edition of *Who's Who in Education*.

In the summer of 1990, Dr. Wong and his wife Ada led an environmental studies delegation to the Soviet Union. The project was co-sponsored by the U.S. Youth Science Ambassador program and the Soviet Academy of Sciences.